Cornerstones of Freedom

African-Americans in the Old West

TOM McGOWEN

CHILDREN'S PRESS®
A Division of Grolier Publishing
New York • London • Hong Kong • Sydney
Danbury, Connecticut

Library of Congress Cataloging-in-Publication Data

McGowen, Tom.
    African-Americans in the Old West / by Tom McGowen.
        p. cm.—(Cornerstones of freedom)
    Includes index.
    Summary: Describes the important role of freed slaves and other
African-Americans in the settlement of the West.
        ISBN: 0-516-20835-7 (lib. bdg.)   0-516-26348-X (pbk.)
        1. Afro-Americans—West (U.S.)—History—Juvenile literature.
2. Frontier and pioneer life—West (U.S.)—Juvenile literature.
3. West (U.S.)—Race relations—Juvenile literature. [1. Afro-
Americans—West (U.S.)—History. 2. West (U.S.)—History.
3. Frontier and pioneer life—West (U.S.)] I. Title. II. Series.
E185.925.M36 1998
978'.00496073—dc21
                                                            97-26583
                                                                 CIP
                                                                 AC

When you think of the words "Old West," what comes to mind? Perhaps you think of cowboys, gunfighters, railroad workers, settlers, soldiers, and American Indians. These were the people who built the Old West. And many of them, from cowboys to soldiers, were African-Americans who had once been slaves.

Many people think of cowboys when they think about the Old West.

One of the first men to explore the West for the United States was an African-American slave. He was known only by the name "York." York was a member of the famous Lewis and Clark Expedition (1804–1806), the first American expedition to explore the United States west of the Missouri River. York was the slave of one of the expedition's leaders, William Clark.

The American Indian tribes that the expedition met were very interested in York. They had never seen anyone like him, and they thought his dark color was painted on! York enjoyed the attention. It was easy for him to make friends with the Indians. The Indians' willingness to

The American Indians were fascinated by York, the only black member of the Lewis and Clark Expedition.

James Beckwourth escaped from slavery, and later discovered the pass that bears his name.

help the expedition made things easier for the explorers. When the expedition was finished in 1806, Clark gave York his freedom.

Another early explorer of the West was also an African-American slave named James Beckwourth. In 1822, he fled from slavery in Missouri and headed west. Beckwourth lived for a time with the Crow Indians, who adopted him. In 1850, he made an important discovery in the mountains between California and Nevada. It was a pass, or opening, through the mountains. In later years, it became the best route for people traveling between Nevada and California. Today, it is known as Beckwourth Pass. A nearby town in California is also named after James Beckwourth.

Southerners believed that their economy would not survive without the use of slave labor on their plantations.

Most of the West was largely unsettled when Beckwourth was there. That began to change about 1865, the year the American Civil War ended. The war, which began in 1861, was fought between the Northern and the Southern states. The Southern way of life was very different from life in the North. The South had slavery. Nearly four million blacks were Southern slaves. Most Northerners were against slavery. The slavery issue so divided the country that the South decided to separate from the North. The Southern states formed their own government, called the Confederate States of America, or the Confederacy. The Confederacy went to war against the Northern states (the Union).

The South lost the war, and the region was devastated. Many of its farms had been ruined. A lot of businesses had shut down. Thousands of men who had been Southern soldiers had come home. They needed jobs, but there were not many jobs available. Many former soldiers decided to leave the South in search of a better life.

In 1863, the U.S. government, led by President Abraham Lincoln, had passed a law called the Emancipation Proclamation that freed the slaves. The slaves were joyful, but they still had many problems. There were almost no jobs for them. Many faced starvation. But little help was given to former slaves. Most white Southerners were angry that the slaves had been freed. Southern states made their own laws that kept the former slaves from really being free. They were cheated, beaten, and sometimes murdered. Things steadily grew worse. In time, many former slaves also decided to leave the South.

Abraham Lincoln issued the Emancipation Proclamation on January 1, 1863.

Most of the former slaves and former soldiers chose to go west. There were only five western states in 1865—Texas, Kansas, Nevada, Oregon, and California. Only a few towns had been established in these states, and those towns had small populations. The rest of the land was government-owned territory. Although American Indians lived in the western lands, much of it was unsettled. It was a tremendous, wide-open place with room for millions of people.

At first, former slaves and former soldiers headed to Texas cattle ranches. During the Civil War, ranch owners had sold cattle to the

By the end of the Civil War, the United States had expanded to include five western states.

Southern armies for food (beef). But once the war was over, ranchers began looking for a way to get their cattle to the East, where beef was in great demand. But there were no railroads in Texas. The cattle had to be herded hundreds of miles north to towns that were connected to the railroad. The Chisholm, Kansas, and Shawnee were a few of the trails that were used. To work on these cattle drives, the ranchers needed cowboys, which created job opportunities in Texas for the former soldiers and freed slaves. The former slaves called the way into Texas the "Freedom Road."

Cattle ranches prospered during the Civil War because the beef they produced was used to feed Southern soldiers.

Freed slaves moved west after the Civil War to become cowboys and ranch hands.

During the Civil War, Texas had been part of the Confederacy. The Texas ranchers had all been slave owners who were forced to free their slaves after the war. As a result, the ranchers didn't like the former slaves. But ranch owners were glad to hire them because freed slaves were willing to work for lower wages than white workers. So, many African-Americans became cowboys. From the 1870s to the 1890s, one of every five cowboys was African-American.

Sometimes, however, problems arose among former Southern soldiers and freed slaves who were working together as cowboys. Some of the white cowboys, whose families had once owned slaves, had difficulty treating former slaves as equals. Black cowboys were usually not allowed to eat in restaurants with white cowboys. African-Americans who spoke out against slavery and Southern ways were often beaten or badly mistreated.

A few African-American cowboys managed to do quite well. Some were able to save enough money to buy their own small ranches and herds of cattle. One, a man named Al Jones, rose to become a trail boss. Twice each year, ranchers had hundreds of their cattle rounded up for shipment east. The trail boss was in charge of the roundup, the cattle drive, and the other cowboys.

To get to the railroads, the cattle drive had to be guided across vast plains, through hilly country, and across rivers. There was always a risk that the herd would suddenly stampede, injuring or killing some of the cowboys. There was also the threat of rustlers (cattle thieves), and the danger of cattle and cowboys drowning as they crossed rivers. Sometimes the danger was from American Indians, who would lie in wait for a cattle drive and demand a payment of cattle to let the drive pass through their territory.

Cattle drives were long, difficult journeys that sometimes took months to complete.

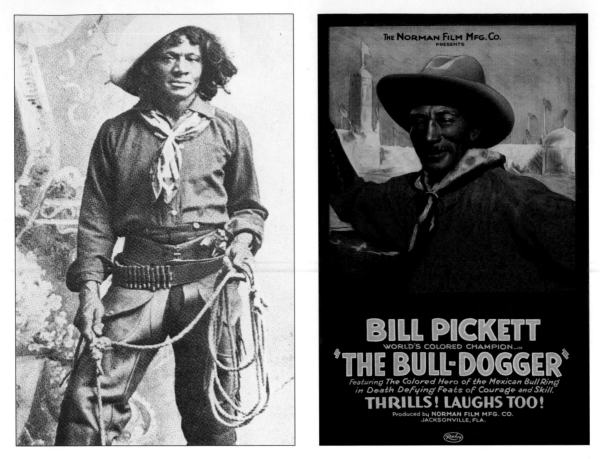

Nat Love (left) and Bill Pickett (right)

A few African-American cowboys became well-known. Nat Love was born into a slave family in Tennessee in 1854. In 1869, at the age of fifteen, he went to Kansas hoping to become a cowboy. He succeeded and lived a life of adventure. He herded cattle, fought outlaws, and was once captured by American-Indian warriors. Eventually, Nat became an author. He wrote a book titled *The Life and Adventures of Nat Love by Himself*. The book made him famous.

Another African-American cowboy, Bill Pickett, was also a former slave. Pickett learned to be a cowboy while growing up on a ranch in

Texas. Years later, he became a rodeo star. Anyone who has ever been to a rodeo—a western-style show featuring cowboys and cowgirls—has seen "bulldogging." In a bulldogging performance, a cowboy jumps from his horse onto the back of a running steer. He grabs the steer by the horns and wrestles it to the ground. Bill Pickett invented bulldogging. He did it for the first time at a rodeo in 1903.

Not all former slaves became cowboys. Most were just ordinary settlers. They settled on a piece of western land and began to farm. Life was often difficult for them. A former slave named Toby once described how he and his wife, Govie, became settlers. They went to Texas in 1869 and settled in a vast empty area. They cut down some trees and built a log hut. To farm, Toby and Govie poked holes in the ground with sharp sticks and dropped corn in. Toby made a bow and arrows and hunted wild animals for food. Govie made clothes out of animal skins. They did not see another person for six years!

Settlers in the West faced many hardships, and African-Americans were no exception.

Many former slaves were able to find various jobs in the West. Some worked laying tracks for the railroads that were being built throughout the West. One former slave earned the first dollar he had ever been paid as a railroad worker. He said it made him feel like the "richest man in the world!"

Some African-Americans became teamsters. They drove wagons loaded with goods from one

This African-American teamster worked in Idaho Springs, Colorado.

place to another, as truck drivers do today. People who did this were called "teamsters" because the wagons were pulled by groups of horses called "teams."

Other former slaves became stagecoach drivers. One of them was a woman named Mary Fields. Some time after the slaves were freed, she traveled West to become a settler. In 1895, at the age of sixty-three, Mary took a job driving a mail coach in Montana. It was a hard job—she often had to drive through blinding blizzards of snow. But Mary could handle it. She was 6 feet (183 centimeters) tall and weighed 200 pounds (91 kilograms). She was known as "Stagecoach Mary," and was noted for smoking cigars as she drove her coach.

Many African-Americans became homesteaders. In 1862, President Abraham Lincoln signed a law called the Homestead Act. The law made it possible for any American citizen to own 160 acres (65 hectares) of land without having to pay for it. If a citizen lived on this land for five years and farmed it, it was his to keep. When slaves were set free and made citizens, many of them took advantage of the Homestead Act. They went to the newest states of Kansas and Nebraska, and the territories of Colorado, Oklahoma, and Utah. There, they settled on government land, built cabins, and started farms, raising corn and vegetables.

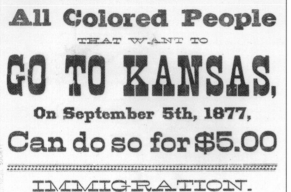

This 1877 handbill from Lexington, Kentucky, announces the formation of a new African-American community that will be settled in Kansas.

In some places, African-American homesteaders became part of growing communities, such as Abilene and Dodge City, in Kansas. In other places, they formed African-American communities of their own. In time, there were nearly thirty such towns in Kansas and twenty-eight in Oklahoma. The people of these towns elected their own mayor, sheriff, and other officials.

In Oklahoma, several thousand African-Americans became homesteaders without even having to move. They had not been slaves to white owners. They were actually slaves of a community of about fifty thousand American Indians known as the Five Tribes. Members of the Cherokee, Choctaw, Chickasaw, Seminole, and Creek formed the Five Tribes. They lived on a reservation in the Oklahoma Territory. The reservation was located between the Southern states of Texas and Arkansas. Both of these states allowed slavery. The Five Tribes decided to own slaves, too. They had more than seven thousand slaves.

Most American Indian tribes took no side during the Civil War. But because the Five Tribes lived between two Southern states, they sided with the South. Some of their warriors even fought against the Northern troops. The U.S. government in Washington, D.C., regarded this action as treason. As punishment, the government took away almost half of the Five Tribes' land when the war was over. The black slaves were set free, and the land was given to them to homestead.

Former slaves continued to move into the West for years after the war. More than ten thousand African-Americans arrived in Kansas between 1870 and 1879. They were called "Exodusters." The name came from the second book of the Bible, Exodus. The word "exodus" means journey. The Exodusters were fleeing from hunger and bad treatment in the South. They

Nicodemus, Kansas—one of the communities settled and run by African-Americans

were so eager to leave the South that many journeyed to Kansas with nothing but the clothes they were wearing. Without the help of white Kansans and American Indians, many of the Exodusters would have starved.

The Wild Bunch included two of the most famous outlaws in the West—Harry Longbaugh (seated, left) and George LeRoy Parker (seated, right). Parker and Longbaugh are better known as Butch Cassidy and the Sundance Kid.

Isom Dart left slavery behind for a life of adventure in the West.

African-Americans who left the South to live in the West were hoping for a better life. But they were often treated badly in the West, too. In many places, they were not allowed to live near white people. In Oklahoma, a law was passed to keep African-American children from going to the same schools as white children. Another law kept African-Americans from being buried in the same cemeteries as whites.

The Old West was known for its outlaws, and some of them were African-American. One of the most famous outlaws was Isom Dart, a former slave. Dart became a railroad worker, a soldier, a rodeo performer—and a cattle thief! He worked for a well-known western outlaw gang known as the Wild Bunch. Isom Dart was a gunslinger, a person noted for skill and speed in handling a gun. But Isom never killed anyone. He was shot to death in Wyoming in 1900 by another gunslinger named Tom Horn.

Cowboys, railroad workers, and settlers certainly played a big part in helping to build the West. But perhaps the biggest part of all was played by soldiers of the U.S. Army. The army protected the settlements and railroads throughout the West. In many places, the soldiers upheld the law against bandits and cattle rustlers. They helped to explore and to map thousands of miles of unknown territory. And they fought many battles against American Indians during the Indian Wars.

African-American soldiers often rode atop stagecoaches to ensure their safe passage through unsafe territory.

From 1865 to 1900, many army regiments were sent to the West. A regiment was an organization of several hundred soldiers. Some were cavalrymen, who fought on horseback. Others were infantrymen, who marched and fought on foot. Regiments stayed for a specific amount of time, then were sent somewhere else. But there were four regiments that stayed in the West for almost thirty years. Before the Civil War, there were no African-Americans in the U.S. Army. Only men who were citizens could join the army, and African-Americans were not considered to be citizens. But during the war a number of black regiments were formed to fight for the North. The men in these regiments were all volunteers. Some of them lived in the North

Black regiments served with pride and distinction during the Civil War.

The 9th Cavalry was one of the first regiments created by the U.S. Army for African-American soldiers.

as free men. Others were slaves who had escaped from the South. These African-American soldiers fought so well that U.S. Army leaders were impressed. As a result, African-American regiments were formed after the war. In 1866, four regiments—the 9th and 10th Cavalry, and the 24th and 25th Infantry—were officially created as part of the U.S. Army. Except for the officers who led them, every soldier in each of these regiments was black.

Establishing the railroad in the West was made more difficult by American-Indian warriors who wanted to stop U.S. expansion into their lands.

The 9th and 10th Cavalry Regiments arrived in the West in 1867. The 9th Cavalry went to Texas; the 10th Cavalry went to Kansas. Less than four months after the 10th Cavalry arrived, the soldiers had their first battle. Their foes were Cheyenne and Arapaho warriors. These tribes had been fighting against the United States government for several years. They were fighting to keep possession of the land that had been theirs for generations. The land was slowly being taken over by settlers, railroads, army forts, and towns. The Indians fought by making quick raids, to do as much damage as they could in a short amount of time. They hoped this strategy would help them to stop the steady takeover of their territory.

On August 1, 1867, the 10th Cavalry received word that warriors had attacked a camp of railroad workers. Thirteen workers had been killed. A small force of thirty-four soldiers rode out to the camp.

Indian raids on settlers and railroad camps were often quick, but deadly.

The next morning, as the soldiers were scouting the land around the camp, they were attacked by a large force of warriors. For two hours, the cavalrymen held off the Indians, who outnumbered them heavily. Then, another large group of warriors joined the attack. The cavalrymen managed to break through the attackers and pulled back. For six more hours, they made a fighting retreat until the Indians finally gave up. The small cavalry force had only one soldier killed and several wounded.

Members of the 10th Cavalry were the first to be called Buffalo Soldiers.

Some time later, the men of the 10th Cavalry learned that the Cheyenne they had fought had given them a nickname—the Buffalo Soldiers.

No one knows exactly why the Cheyenne called the men of the 10th Cavalry Buffalo Soldiers. But the name was not an insult. The Cheyenne, like most Plains Indians, regarded the buffalo as a noble, sacred animal. Perhaps the Indians gave the soldiers the name because the soldiers had fought so fiercely when they were surrounded by the Indians, just as buffalo would. They meant the name as a compliment. The men of the 10th Cavalry accepted the nickname proudly. Before long, both the 10th and 9th Cavalry were known throughout the West as Buffalo Soldiers.

In Texas, the 9th Cavalry's foes were the Commanche, Kiowa, and Apache, as well as Mexican bandits. The soldiers were split up into two groups to guard against raids. In 1876, the 9th Cavalry spent months chasing Apache raiders led by the famous chief, Geronimo. By this time, the 24th and 25th Infantry had also been sent to the West. They often fought alongside the cavalry against the Indians. They, too, became known as Buffalo Soldiers.

The African-American regiments had their own customs. Some were left over from the time they spent as slaves. One of the few pleasures slaves had was music, especially singing. The Buffalo Soldiers, too, were fond of music. They often sang as they were riding, marching, working, or relaxing. They sang as well as a professional chorus. Once, a group of soldiers of the 25th Infantry was ordered to stay in their barracks. This was a punishment, similar to being in jail. With nothing else to do, the soldiers began to sing. Their singing was so beautiful, that the officer who had ordered their punishment decided to release them from their barracks!

Geronimo, the legendary Apache chief who fought the U.S. Army for more than ten years until his capture in 1876.

Above: Lt. Henry O. Flipper

Below: African-American soldiers often received poor quality supplies and equipment.

In 1878, the Buffalo Soldiers were given their first African-American officer. He was Second Lieutenant Henry O. Flipper, the first African-American to graduate from the United States Military Academy at West Point. Flipper was the only African-American officer in the entire U.S. Army. He was assigned to the 10th Cavalry, which was then stationed in Texas.

Lieutenant Flipper did his job well for several years. Then, he was accused of committing a crime. A military court found him not guilty, but he was forced to resign from the army. He stayed in the West and became a successful mining engineer. In his later life, he was appointed to a high position in the U.S. government.

The Buffalo Soldiers were protecting the lives and property of the people of the West, risking their own lives to do so. Yet even the U.S. Army did not treat the Buffalo Soldiers well. Most of the equipment they were given—saddles, blankets, tents, etc.—was old and worn. The soldiers were also given horses that were usually too old, or were lame (unable to walk properly due to an injury or disease). Some of the buildings that the soldiers lived in were falling apart. The soldiers' food was not very good, either. Many of the white officers complained, but nothing changed.

Despite the poor treatment they were given, the Buffalo Soldiers did their duties well. When called upon to fight, they fought bravely. During the time the four regiments spent in the West, fourteen African-American soldiers were awarded the Army Medal of Honor. This is the highest award that can be given to an American soldier. It is given for extreme bravery in battle.

The Army Medal of Honor, first awarded in 1863, is the highest award for bravery given by the U.S. Army.

Seminole-Negro Indians were also commended by the U.S. Army for their expert scouting and tracking abilities.

Four other soldiers of African ancestry were also given the Medal of Honor at that time. These men were actually both African-American and American Indian. The Seminole Indians had lived in Florida, and since the 1700s had given shelter to escaped slaves from all over the South. Thousands of runaway slaves had joined the Seminole over the years. Many African-Americans had married Seminole. In time, most people of the tribe had mixed ancestry. They were known as Black Indians, and were excellent scouts and trackers. The U.S. Army hired many of them after the Civil War. They formed a unit called the Seminole-Negro Indian Scouts. It was four men of this unit who received the Medal of Honor while serving in Texas.

By 1900, the Indian Wars had come to an end. Farms, towns, and bustling cities dotted the now peaceful prairies. Trains chugged steadily over railroad tracks. Nine new states had been created—Nebraska, North Dakota, South Dakota, Montana, Wyoming, Colorado, Idaho, Utah, and Washington. Three more—Oklahoma, Arizona, and New Mexico—would be established within the next twelve years. The time of the "Old West" was over. The West had become an important part of the United States. And cowboys, settlers, railroad workers, and soldiers, many of whom were African-Americans, all played important roles in building it.

As the United States continued to grow in the 1900s, fewer soldiers were needed to protect the prairies. Still, African-Americans are remembered as instrumental figures in the growth of the American West.

GLOSSARY

bandit – an armed robber, usually a member of a gang

barracks – buildings where soldiers live

chorus – large group of people who sing together

foe – enemy

hut – small, primitive house

hut

outlaw – a criminal, especially one who is running away from the law

scout – someone sent to find out and bring back information

stampede – sudden scattering of cattle or horses in fright

strategy – plan for winning a military battle or achieving a goal

territory – part of the United States that is not yet admitted as a state

tracker – person who follows the marks or prints left behind by a moving person or animal

tracker

treason – the crime of betraying your country by spying for another country or by helping an enemy during a war

veteran – someone who has served in the armed forces, especially during a war

volunteer – someone who offers to do a job, usually without pay

TIMELINE

1804

York becomes
member of
Lewis and Clark
expedition

1822 James Beckwourth explores the West

1861

Lincoln signs Homestead Act **1862**

Lincoln signs Emancipation Proclamation **1863**

Indian Wars begin **1865**

} American Civil War

Cavalry, infantry regiments arrive in West **1867**

Nat Love becomes cowboy **1869**

1870

} Exodusters arrive in Kansas

1879

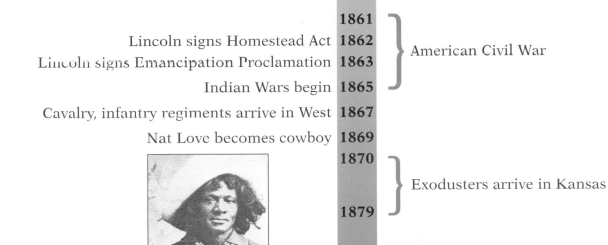

1895 Mary Fields becomes "Stagecoach Mary"

1900 Indian Wars end

DEDICATION

To my friends Dorothy Evans, Glennette Turner, Harriet Robinet, and Darwin Walton

INDEX (*Boldface* page numbers indicate illustrations.)

PHOTO CREDITS

ABOUT THE AUTHOR

Tom McGowen is a children's author with special interest in the Old West and in military history. He lives in Norridge, Illinois, and is the author of forty-seven books on various subjects for young readers. In 1990, Mr. McGowen won the Children's Reading Roundtable Award for Outstanding Contribution to the Field of Juvenile Literature.